contents

Key

Number and Place Value

Addition and Subtraction

Multiplication and Division

Shape, Data and Measure

Fractions and Decimals

Mixed Operations

How to use this book

The first page of each section will have a title telling you what the next few pages are about.

Some pages will show you an example or model.

Sometimes a character will give you a tip.

Read the instructions carefully before each set of questions.

Column addition and subtraction

Perform these additions using the column method.

| 1 | 35 284 + 12 461 | 30 000 5000 200 80 4 + 10 000 2000 400 60 1 |

You can write out these additions compact or expanded.

| 2 | 53 164 + 31 263 |
| 5 | 25 674 + 35 251 |

| 3 | 28 341 + 42 025 |
| 6 | 19 875 + 42 312 |

| 4 | 51 963 + 26 320 |
| 7 | 41 759 + 16 421 |

8	22 221 17 316 + 3 142
9	31 372 40 601 + 5 414
10	12 921 231 92 + 4 012

THINK Write an addition of two 5-digit numbers where every digit is different. What is the largest total you can make?

○○○ I am confident with adding 5-digit numbers using column addition.

38

Perform these additions using the column method.

1	46 825 + 19 041
3	38 421 + 40 593
5	53 296 + 46 345

2	52 319 + 25 920
4	42 861 + 38 412
6	26 139 + 67 408

7	17 245 59 652 + 1 031
9	31 632 37 541 + 5 235
11	21 480 64 271 + 17 155

8	62 418 13 646 + 4 101
10	48 217 12 426 + 33 145
12	30 240 45 918 + 27 514

THINK Write an addition of two 5-digit numbers where every digit is different. What is the largest total you can make? What is the smallest total you can make? Can you make 22 221 if one of the two numbers has 4 digits?

○○○ I am confident with adding 5-digit numbers using column addition.

39

THINK questions will challenge you to think more about the maths on the page.

Each area of maths has its own colour.

Choose a traffic light colour to say how confident you are with the maths on the page.

Adding and subtracting money

Complete these additions.

 **THINK** Look at the additions below. Which will have the biggest answer? Which will have the smallest answer? Which addition do you think will have an answer closest to £5?

① £4·30 + 40p + £2 = ☐

② £5·90 + £1·10 + 35p = ☐

③ £5·20 + £2·80 + 30p = ☐

④ £1·80 + £2·20 + 99p = ☐

⑤ £3·40 + £1·60 + 77p = ☐

⑥ £4·30 + £1·70 + 48p = ☐

⑦ £2·50 + 39p + £2·50 = ☐

⑧ £1·05 + 95p + £1·60 = ☐

Solve this word problem.

⑨ Kate goes to the farmers' market. She buys a punnet of strawberries for £2·50, a nectarine for 60p and a mango for £1·20. How much does she spend altogether?

£2·50

60p

£1·20

○
○ **I am confident with adding amounts of money using**
○ **mental methods.**

Complete these additions.

 Estimate each total amount before working out each addition.

1 £6·80 + 35p + 90p = ☐

4 £3·70 + £4·50 + 67p = ☐

2 £2·40 + £3·99 + 50p = ☐

5 £5·90 + 82p + £2·90 = ☐

3 £7·30 + 56p + £2·70 = ☐

6 £4·99 + £3·70 + 60p = ☐

Solve these word problems.

7 Paige went to the shop and bought a puzzle magazine for 95p, a mini-torch for £3·05 and a packet of sweets for 69p. How much did Paige spend altogether?

8 Tommy and Francis went to an art shop. They bought a paintbrush for 88p, some origami paper for £3·10 and a set of paints for £4·02. How much did they spend altogether?

9 Mia runs a market stall. One day, her first customer bought a necklace for £4·60 and a gift bag for 40p. Mia's second customer spent £4·75 on a ring. How much money did Mia make that day?

♥ Mia's Jewellery ★

○
○ **I am confident with adding amounts of money**
○ **using mental methods.**

5

Complete these additions.

Can you see any near numbers or number bonds?

1 £5·25 + £1·99 + £1·75 = ☐

2 £7·20 + £1·40 + 79p = ☐

3 £5·55 + 80p + £2·90 = ☐

4 £1·80 + 75p + £6·20 + 75p = ☐

5 £2·60 + 60p + £3·40 + 45p = ☐

6 £3·99 + £2·99 + 60p + 70p = ☐

7 99p + £1·70 + £3·90 + 20p = ☐

8 £3·70 + 43p + £6·95 + 57p = ☐

Solve these word problems.

9 Jennie and Temuri went to a street-food market. Jennie chose some olives for £1·90 and some chilli sauce for £2·99. Temuri chose three cakes that were 65p each. How much did Jennie and Temuri spend altogether?

10 David is running the jar stall at the school fete. Phillippe buys a jar of sweets for £1·55, some homemade honey for £4·85 and a jar of beans for 77p. He pays with a £10 note. How much change does David give him?

THINK Paul buys three things, each costing an amount that ends in 99p. He spends 3p less than £7. What could each of the items cost?

○
○ **I am confident with adding amounts of money**
○ **using mental methods.**

You have £20. Work out how much change you would get if you bought:

 1

2

 3

4

You have £50. Work out how much change you would get if you bought a family ticket for:

5

7

6
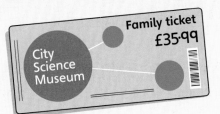

8

THINK Charlie has £14·14 in his wallet. He buys a book costing £ ☐ ·99 and a drink costing £ ☐ ·50. He has £6·65 left. What could the book and drink have cost?

I am confident with subtracting amounts of money using mental methods.

You have £50. Work out how much change you would get if you bought:

1 Annual Fireworks Concert Ticket £32.70

2 In concert ★ FAR OUT SHERRIFF at the City Arena £28.90

3 Festival in a field LIVE MUSIC · CIRCUS · FOOD STALLS · CAMPING Weekend ticket: £35.50

Complete these subtractions.

4 £18·50 – £7·99 = ☐

5 £25·40 – £13·20 = ☐

6 £44·75 – £19·25 = ☐

Solve these problems.

7 Ahmed earned £84·60 washing cars. He decided to get a new game for his console for £44·99. How much money will he have left?

8 Connor had £48·30 in his money box but spent £27·10 of it. Mel had £34·30 in her money box but spent £11·40 of it. Who has more money left after their spending? How much do they each have?

THINK Laura spends £2·99 on a drink, and double this amount on a burger. She has three non-brown coins, which are all different, left in her purse after she has bought the items. What different amounts could she have started with?

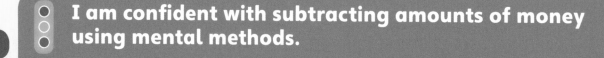

Find the change from £10.

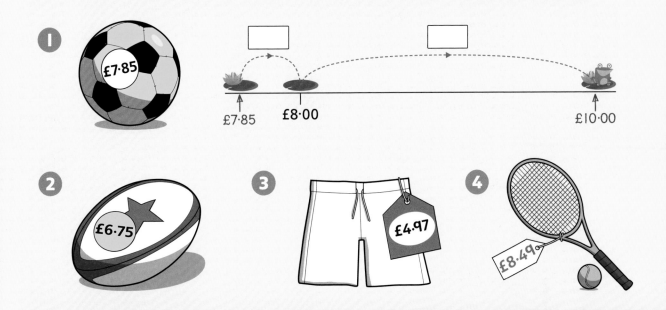

1. £7·85

£7·85   £8·00   £10·00

2. £6·75

3. £4·97

4. £8·49

Find the change from £20.

5. £12·75

7. ABC DICTIONARY £13·45

9. SPACE RACE £14·49

6. £15·70

8. £11·89

10. £16·82

THINK Choose two of the answers from this page. Draw the smallest amount of coins you can use to make the amount of change.

○
○ **I am confident with subtracting amounts of money**
○ **using counting up.**

Copy this table. Estimate the answer for each question on this page.

Question number	More than £5	Less than £5
1	✔	
2		
3		
4		
5		
6		
7		
8		
9		
10		

Work out the change you would get from £20.

1 MOUNTAIN EXPRESS
Adult
From HILL STN
To MOUNTAIN STN
Price £14·82

2 MOUNTAIN EXPRESS
Adult
From FOREST STN
To MOUNTAIN STN
Price £11·26

3 MOUNTAIN EXPRESS
Adult
From PLAIN STN
To MOUNTAIN STN
Price £9·65

4 MOUNTAIN EXPRESS
Adult
From CANYON STN
To MOUNTAIN STN
Price £13·77

5 MOUNTAIN EXPRESS
Adult
From COAST STN
To MOUNTAIN STN
Price £15·34

6 MOUNTAIN EXPRESS
Adult
From VALLEY STN
To MOUNTAIN STN
Price £16·11

Work out the amount each child has left in their online music download accounts.

Use Frog to work these out. You will need three jumps.

7 Mary has £18·23 and spends £11·38.

8 Troy has £24·35 and spends £15·90.

9 Lei has £12·84 and spends £3·95.

10 Asma has £31·44 and spends £20·57.

○
○ **I am confident with subtracting amounts**
○ **of money using counting up.**

calculations using mental methods

Solve these word problems.

1. Amelia bought some flowers for her mum. She paid £4·60 for tulips and £2·70 for daffodils. How much did she spend altogether?

2. Zoya bought a CD for £7·79 for her dad. How much change did she get from £10?

3. For her mum's birthday, Susie bought a necklace costing £12·00. She also bought a gift box for £2·99. How much did she spend?

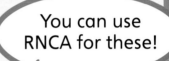

You can use RNCA for these!

4. Claire bought two mugs for her younger twin brothers. Each mug cost £4·60. How much did they both cost together?

5. Piotr bought a DVD for £11·49 for his brother. How much change did he get from £20?

6. Alfie spent £32·70 of his £50 birthday money on a new bike. How much change did he get from £50?

7. Nate was given money for his birthday. His aunt gave him £40, his sister gave him £10 and his mum gave him £50. Nate bought a computer game for £43·90. How much money did he have left to spend after this?

 **THINK** Mark has £10 to buy his dad a present. He wants to buy a mug for £4·99 and a box of chocolates for £2·50. Does he have enough to also buy a card for £2·70?

○
○ **I am confident with solving problems involving**
○ **subtracting and adding money using mental methods.**

1 Laura spends £1·75 on a birthday card and £1·99 on wrapping paper for her mum's birthday present. How much does she spend altogether?

2 An adult ticket for a football match costs £3·80 more than a child's ticket. If the child's ticket costs £14·60, how much does the adult ticket cost?

3 Sue saw a book she liked for £7·99. In the sale it was reduced by £2·49. What was the reduced price of the book?

4 Sam has £27·13 in his wallet. He buys a DVD for £14·99. How much money does he have left?

5 Parveen went to the cinema. She spent £4·25 on her ticket, £2·50 on popcorn and £1·20 on a bottle of water. How much change did she get from £10?

6 At a theme park the entrance fees are £4 for a child and £8·50 for an adult. Rides cost £3 each. If a man and his 10-year-old son have £25 to spend in total, how many rides can they go on after paying the entrance fees?

7 A bookshop has a sale. Books that cost £7·49 are reduced by £3·99. How much does it cost to buy two of these books in the sale?

8 Books that cost £8·99 are reduced by £2·50. How much change from £20 does Min get if he buys three of these books in the sale?

Write a word problem for your partner. It must be one that makes them do two separate calculations.

○
○ **I am confident with solving problems involving**
○ **subtracting and adding money using**
  mental methods.

Solve these word problems.

1 Zara had £20. She bought a cake for her grandad's birthday party. It cost £4·85. Zara also bought him a present for £7·95 and wrapping paper for 40p. How much money does she have left?

2 Maria was given a charm bracelet for her birthday. Her sister gave her three charms which cost £8·99 each. She bought a gift box to put the charms in, which cost £2. How much did Maria's sister spend altogether?

3 Tom has £9·53 in his money box and £14·14 in his wallet. He wants to buy a present for his mum that costs £24·99. Does he have enough money and, if not, how much more will he need?

4 For her birthday Sadie was given a new bike and £30 in spending money. She went shopping with the money and bought a cycle helmet for £14·34 and a pair of gloves for £6. Does she have enough money left to buy shin pads that cost £9·50?

5 Isabella went to a football match. She bought a programme for £3·50, a drink for £2·99 and a pie for £2·40. If she went home with £7·25, how much money did she take to the match?

6 Abshly wants to buy a box-set of his favourite TV series. He sees it in a shop for £29·99 but with £2 off in a sale. He looks online and finds the same series for £22·48 plus £4·99 delivery. Which option is cheaper and by how much?

 Write a word problem for your partner. It must be one that makes them do one addition and one subtraction.

I am confident with solving problems involving subtracting and adding money using mental methods.

Multiplying fractions

Double the fractions below. Write your answers as mixed numbers. Simplify the fractions where you can.

1. $\dfrac{2}{5}$

2. $\dfrac{3}{4}$

3. $\dfrac{3}{8}$

4. $\dfrac{4}{5}$

5. $\dfrac{1}{4}$

6. $\dfrac{7}{8}$

Multiply these fractions by 3.

7. $\dfrac{2}{3}$

8. $\dfrac{2}{5}$

9. $\dfrac{3}{4}$

10. $\dfrac{2}{7}$

11. $\dfrac{4}{5}$

12. $\dfrac{3}{7}$

Multiply these fractions by 4.

13. $\dfrac{2}{3}$

14. $\dfrac{1}{4}$

15. $\dfrac{2}{7}$

16. $\dfrac{3}{5}$

17. $\dfrac{5}{6}$

18. $\dfrac{2}{6}$

Multiply these fractions by 5.

19. $\dfrac{13}{6}$

20. $\dfrac{10}{8}$

21. $\dfrac{4}{7}$

22. $\dfrac{6}{6}$

23. $\dfrac{12}{4}$

24. $\dfrac{11}{5}$

 **THINK** Write a multiplication of a whole number by a fraction. It should give a whole number answer.

 I am confident with multiplying fractions by a whole number.

Short multiplication

Perform these multiplications using the ladder method.

1
```
   2118
×     4
_____
```

2
```
   3207
×     3
_____
```

3
```
   2627
×     4
_____
```

4
```
   2117
×     5
_____
```

5
```
   3814
×     3
_____
```

6
```
   1241
×     8
_____
```

7
```
   3416
×     4
_____
```

8
```
   5259
×     3
_____
```

9
```
   2616
×     5
_____
```

10
```
   9243
×     3
_____
```

11
```
   3182
×     6
_____
```

12
```
   9013
×     7
_____
```

 **THINK** Work out the missing digits in 3 ☐ 42 × 6 = ☐ 8 852. The two digits are the same. Check that your answer works.

○ **I am confident with using the ladder method to**
○ **perform multiplications.**

Perform these multiplications. Estimate the answers first.

1. 4312
    ×   6

2. 5473
    ×   4

3. 3627
    ×   5

4. 4263
    ×   4

5. 3725
    ×   4

6. 4368
    ×   3

7. 5274
    ×   6

8. 3429
    ×   4

9. 1438
    ×   7

10. 2546
    ×   8

11. 3472
    ×   5

12. 4135
    ×   6

13. 1382
    ×   6

14. 2047
    ×   6

15. 1943
    ×   6

16. 2264
    ×   6

17. 1783
    ×   6

18. 1452
    ×   6

 Use number cards 1–9. Create a 4-digit number and a 1-digit number. Now multiply them together. Investigate how many multiplications you can create with an answer between 8000 and 9000.

I am confident with using short multiplication to perform calculations.

16

Multiplying using the grid method

Use the methods shown to perform these multiplications.

1   24 × 13 = ☐

×	10	3
20	200	60
4	40	12

260
+ 52 = ☐

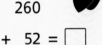

Add each row together. Then add the totals.

2   35 × 13 = ☐

3   42 × 14 = ☐

4   38 × 15 = ☐

5   29 × 16 = ☐

6   61 × 17 = ☐

7   57 × 18 = ☐

8   45 × 22 = ☐

×	20	2
40	800	80
5	100	10

880
+ 110 = ☐

9   43 × 21 = ☐

10   51 × 23 = ☐

11   38 × 31 = ☐

12   52 × 24 = ☐

13   63 × 33 = ☐

14   46 × 42 = ☐

THINK

46 × ☐3 = 598

What is the missing digit?

I am confident with multiplying using the grid method.

Long multiplication

The first part of each question has been done!

Copy and complete these multiplications.

1.
```
    32
×   14
   320

   ___
```

2.
```
    44
×   13
   440

   ___
```

3.
```
    28
×   16
   280

   ___
```

4.
```
    56
×   19
   560

   ___
```

5.
```
   231
×   13
  2310

   ___
```

6.
```
   124
×   14
  1240

   ___
```

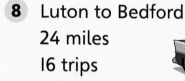

Calculate the total miles each vehicle travels.

7. London to Oxford
52 miles
13 trips

8. Luton to Bedford
24 miles
16 trips

9. Leeds to Hull
68 miles
15 trips

10. London to Paris
213 miles
14 trips

11. Rome to Berlin
732 miles
13 trips

12. Vienna to Dublin
821 miles
16 trips

THINK Does 32 × 16 give you the same answer as 36 × 12?

I am confident with using long multiplication for 2-digit and 3-digit calculations.

Perform these multiplications. Estimate the answers first.

1. 432
    × 14
    ———

2. 135
    × 13
    ———

3. 212
    × 16
    ———

4. 385
    × 15
    ———

5. 843
    × 17
    ———

6. 674
    × 19
    ———

7. 626
    × 18
    ———

8. 748
    × 14
    ———

Solve these word problems.

9. A group of 12 people go on holiday. The holiday costs £124 per person. How much does the holiday cost altogether?

10. A pilot flies from London to Paris and back, which is a total of 426 miles. She does this journey 13 times. How many miles has she flown altogether?

6 ☐ 4 × ☐ 3 = 7982
What are the missing digits?
The two digits are the same.

I am confident with using long multiplication for 2-digit and 3-digit calculations.

Perform these multiplications.

1
```
   548
×   12
_____
```

2
```
   217
×   15
_____
```

3
```
   147
×   13
_____
```

4
```
   571
×   14
_____
```

5
```
   286
×   16
_____
```

6
```
   777
×   18
_____
```

Solve these word problems.

7 A train driver makes 14 journeys, each 312 miles long. How many miles does she travel in total?

8 Some supermarket workers unpack 452 boxes of baked beans, each containing 16 tins. How many tins in total is this?

THINK A 3-digit number that does not end in 0 is multiplied by a 2-digit number that is between 12 and 19. The product is a multiple of 50. Write a multiplication that works.

I am confident with using long multiplication to solve problems.

Solve these multiplications.

1
```
    678
×    16
───────
```

4
```
    708
×    18
───────
```

7
```
    636
×    26
───────
```

2
```
    926
×    17
───────
```

5
```
    488
×    16
───────
```

8
```
    164
×    28
───────
```

3
```
    689
×    19
───────
```

6
```
    793
×    17
───────
```

Six children took part in a multiplication challenge. Here are their answers. Who got one correct? Who got both correct?

9

 Tim

573 × 14 = 8022	684 × 18 = 12 132

 Ranjit

967 × 14 = 12 538	268 × 19 = 5073

 Su Li

826 × 16 = 13 216	386 × 17 = 6562

 Jenny

536 × 16 = 8576	883 × 17 = 15 011

 Jack

845 × 17 = 13 365	573 × 16 = 5968

 Devi

724 × 18 = 13 132	919 × 15 = 13 785

 **THINK** 2 ☐ 1 is multiplied by a teens number between 12 and 20. The product ends in 99. Write a multiplication it could be.

● ● ● **I am confident with using long multiplication to solve problems.**

21

3-place decimal numbers

Compare these decimal numbers.
Write < or > between each pair.

① 2·743   6·115   ④ 4·516   7·064

② 0·625   0·817   ⑤ 0·302   0·203

③ 0·919   0·482   ⑥ 0·529   0·597

Write these decimal numbers in figures.

⑦ One one, nine tenths, three hundredths, two thousandths.

⑧ Six ones, four tenths, one hundredth, seven thousandths.

⑨ Zero ones, eight tenths, five hundredths, one thousandth.

⑩ Two ones, three tenths, eight thousandths.

⑪ Six hundredths, two tenths, three ones, four thousandths.

⑫ Seven thousandths, two tenths, seven ones, three hundredths.

 **THINK** How many 3-place decimal numbers come between 0·23 and 0·24? Write them all down.

Compare these decimal numbers. Write < or > between each pair.

1. 0·672   0·626

2. 0·404   0·401

3. 0·742   7·402

4. 6·635   6·351

5. 5·701   5·071

6. 9·332   9·233

Write these decimal numbers in figures.

7. Three ones, four tenths, one hundredth, eight thousandths.

8. Two ones, four hundredths, nine thousandths.

9. Six ones, five tenths, two thousandths.

10. Seven ones, seven thousandths.

11. Six ones, seven thousandths, three tenths.

12. Five ones, five tenths, one thousandth.

13. Three tenths, five hundredths, seven thousandths.

Write these numbers in order from smallest to largest.

14. 0·382,   0·791,   0·452

15. 2·167,   0·285,   1·266

 Which 3-place decimal number comes halfway between 0·97 and 1·07?

○ **I am confident with reading and writing decimal numbers.**

Write the value of each letter as a 2-place decimal.

Look to see if it is more or less than halfway between two 0·1 markers.

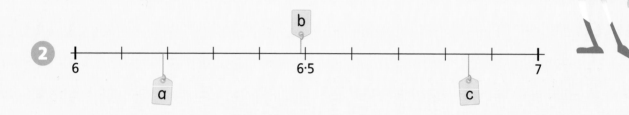

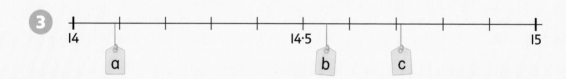

Round these numbers to the nearest tenth.

4 0·68

5 2·41

6 7·52

7 1·73

8 14·89

9 11·82

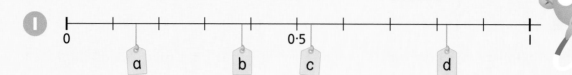

THINK How many 1-place decimal numbers round to 1?

○
○ **I am confident with ordering and rounding**
○ **decimal numbers.**

Write the value of each letter as a 2-place decimal.

1

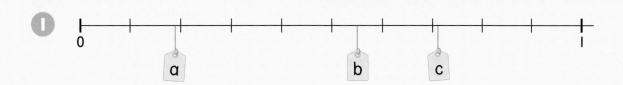

2

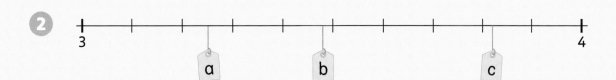

3

4

Round these numbers to the nearest tenth.

5 0·62

6 1·48

7 12·83

8 16·19

9 14·14

10 7·31

 **THINK** Write all the 2-place decimal numbers that round to 2·5.

I am confident with ordering and rounding decimal numbers.

25

Follow these instructions to show decimal numbers on number lines.

1. Draw a number line between 0 and 1.
   Mark on: 0·45, 0·68 and 0·91.

2. Draw a number line between 15 and 16.
   Mark on: 15·75, 15·32 and 15·01.

3. Draw a number line between 3·5 and 4·5.
   Mark on: 3·85, 4·17 and 4·34.

Round these numbers to the nearest tenth.

4. 0·57

6. 8·81

8. 4·16

5. 12·25

7. 13·38

9. 15·54

> Which digits mean you have to round up?

Round these numbers to the nearest hundredth.

10. 0·621

12. 0·123

11. 0·876

13. 0·465

 **THINK** If you write out every number between 0 and 1 as a 2-place decimal, how many round down to 0? How many round up to 1?

I am confident with ordering and rounding decimal numbers.

Jennie has been sent a mystery parcel. She must work out its weight before she can open it. She has the following information.

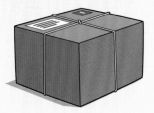

- The parcel's weight is greater than 0 kg and less than 1 kg.
- Written in kilograms, the parcel's weight is a 3-place decimal whose thousandths digit is not zero.
- The weight includes at least one digit that is a 5.

1 Work out how many possible weights match the information above.

> Look at the table and draw a similar one with as many rows as you need to show your findings.

1s	$\frac{1}{10}$ (0·1s)	$\frac{1}{100}$ (0·01s)	$\frac{1}{1000}$ (0·001s)
0	5	0	1
0	5	0	2
0	5		

2 Jennie is given more information. The parcel has a weight that has exactly two 5s in it. Work out how many possible weights now match the information you have.

3 Finally Jennie is given more information. The grams part of the weight has two 5s and a zero. The zero is not in the tenths place. What is the weight of the parcel? Write your answer in kilograms and then in grams.

○
○ **I am confident with solving problems using**
○ **decimal numbers.**

Negative numbers

Write < or > between the pairs of numbers.

1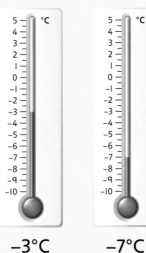

−3°C   −7°C

2

−2°C   −9°C

3 −4°C   2°C

4 −5°C   4°C

5 6°C   −6°C

6 −12°C   −9°C

Write the difference between these temperatures.

7

8

9

THINK

The temperature falls from ☐ °C to −10°C.
If it falls less than 4 degrees, what temperature could it have been to begin with?

○
○ **I am confident with ordering negative and**
○ **positive numbers.**

Compare these temperatures. Write < or > between each pair.

① −7°C   −9°C   ③ −1°C   4°C

② −6°C   −3°C   ④ −8°C   2°C

Write these temperatures in order from coldest to hottest.

⑤ −6°C, −12°C, 5°C   ⑧ 17°C, −4°C, −1°C

⑥ 14°C, 0°C, −7°C   ⑨ 7°C, 10°C, −10°C

⑦ 21°C, −12°C, −2°C   ⑩ −6°C, −1°C, 16°C

Find the difference between these temperatures.

⑪ −2°C and 4°C   ⑬ −1°C and 13°C

⑫ −7°C and 3°C   ⑭ −12°C and −3°C

The temperature falls from ☐ °C to −10°C. If it starts below 0°C, how many different-sized whole number drops could there be? For example, it could drop from −3°C to −10°C, which is a drop of 7°C.

Translations and reflections

Write the coordinates of each shape. Follow the instructions. Write the new coordinates of the vertices.

1
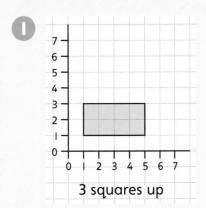
3 squares up

4
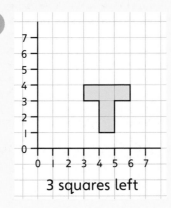
3 squares left

2
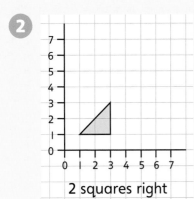
2 squares right

5
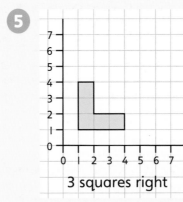
3 squares right

7
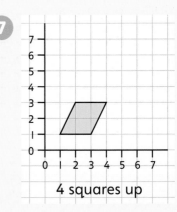
4 squares up

3
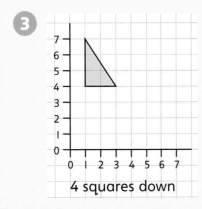
4 squares down

6
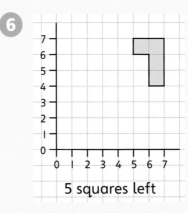
5 squares left

8
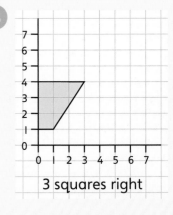
3 squares right

THINK Draw a kite with the coordinates (2,1), (1,3), (3,3) and (2,4). Add 2 to all the y-coordinates and add 1 to all the x-coordinates. What happens to the kite?

○
○ **I am confident with using coordinates and**
○ **translating shapes.**

1 Draw a coordinate grid on cm squared paper. Mark both axes with numbers from 0 to 12.

2 Mark the points (1,1), (2,4), (4,4) and (5,1) and join them. What shape does it make?

3 Add 3 to each of the *y*-coordinates given above. Write the four new pairs of coordinates.

4 Use a coloured pen or pencil to mark the new points on your grid and join them. What happens?

5 Add 2 to the *x*-coordinates of your answers to question 3.

6 Use a different coloured pen or pencil to mark on the new points and join them. Describe what happens to the shape now.

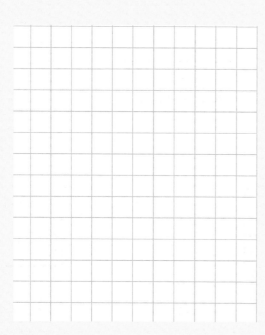

 Write some rules explaining how to translate shapes. How do you move a shape up? How do you move a shape across?

I am confident with translating shapes.

Copy these shapes onto squared paper. Reflect each shape in the y-axis. Write the new coordinates.

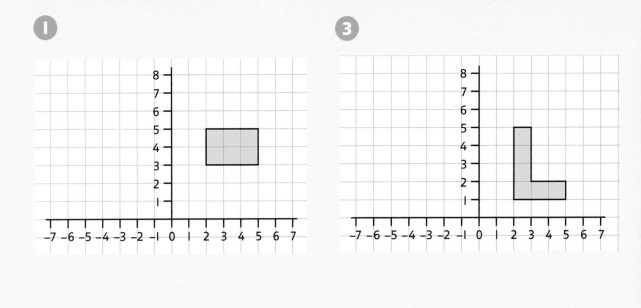

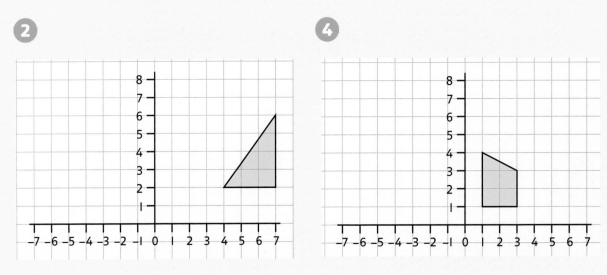

 The coordinates of a square are (2,2), (2,1), (3,1) and (3,2). Write the coordinates of the new square when it has been reflected in the y-axis.

● I am confident with reflecting shapes.
○
○
○

Follow the instructions to help you draw and reflect a polygon.

1. Draw a two-quadrant graph like this one.

2. Mark the positive and negative numbers along the *x*-axis.

3. Mark the *y*-axis with positive numbers going up.

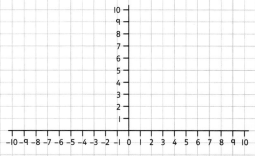

4. Draw a polygon to the right of the *y*-axis, in the positive quadrant.

5. Write the coordinates of your polygon in a list.

6. Write a new list of coordinates where the *x*-coordinate is the negative value of the *x*-coordinate in your first list.

7. Plot these coordinates and draw the shape to the left of the *y*-axis, in the negative quadrant.

8. Use a mirror to check that your new shape is a reflection of your first shape.

Now try this challenge activity.

9. Draw a new graph with just one quadrant. Plot these points: (1, 1), (4, 1), (4, 5) and join them to create a right-angled triangle.

10. Draw a vertical line parallel with the *y*-axis which runs through the point (5, 0).

11. Reflect the shape in this line. Write the coordinates of the new shape.

THINK Is there a relationship between the coordinates of the two shapes in the challenge activity?

○ **I am confident with drawing and reflecting polygons.**

33

Copy the graph and shape. Write the shape's coordinates and reflect it in the y-axis. Write the new coordinates. Repeat this for each graph.

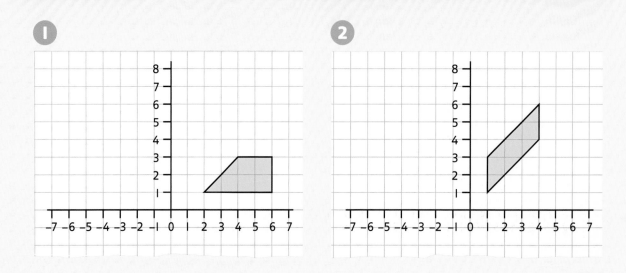

① ②

Copy the graph, shape and line. Write the coordinates of the shape. Draw a reflection of the triangle in the line. Write the new coordinates. Repeat this for each graph.

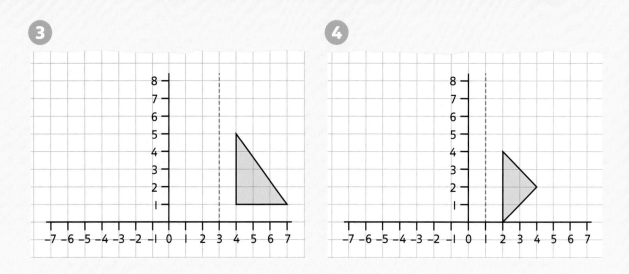

③ ④

 Explain to a partner how the x-coordinates have changed in each shape.

I am confident with drawing and reflecting shapes.

Copy the graph and shape. Write the shape's coordinates and reflect it in the y-axis. Write the new coordinates. Repeat this for each graph.

1

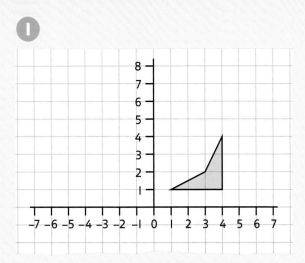

2

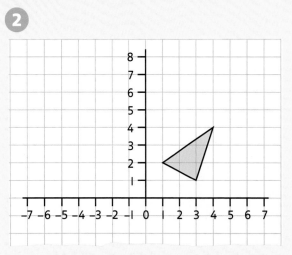

Copy the graph, shape and line. Write the coordinates of the shape. Draw a reflection of the shape in the line. Write the new coordinates. Repeat this for each graph.

3

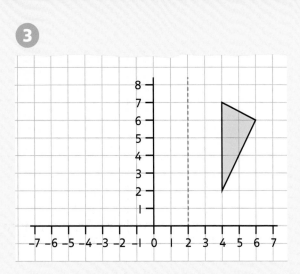

4

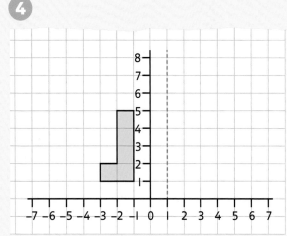

 Explain to a partner how the x-coordinates have changed in each shape.

● I am confident with drawing and reflecting shapes.
○
○
○

Identifying 3D Shapes

Match each 3D shape to the net drawing and to the shape name.

1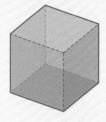

A.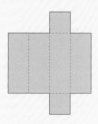

square-based pyramid

2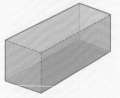

B.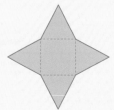

cube

3

C.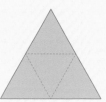

triangular prism

4

D.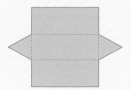

cuboid

5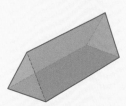

E.

tetrahedron

THINK Draw a net of a cube that does not look like the one above.

○ **I am confident with identifying 3D shapes.**
○
○

Write the shape each net will make. Choose from these shape names.

cuboid   cube

tetrahedron

square-based pyramid

triangular prism

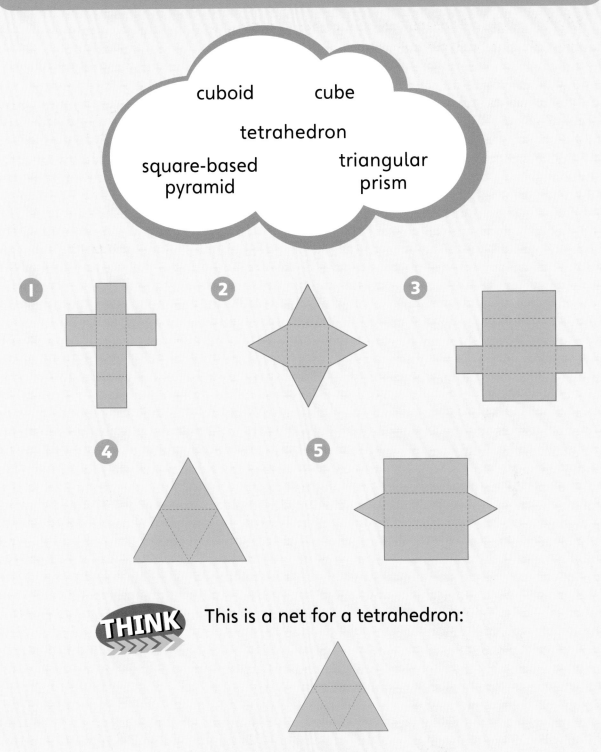

1

2

3

4

5

THINK   This is a net for a tetrahedron:

Draw another one.
How many more can you draw?

Column addition and subtraction

Perform these additions using the column method.

Choose to write these out as compact or expanded addition.

①
```
   35 284
 + 12 461
 _____
```

```
   30 000  5000  200  80  4
 + 10 000  2000  400  60  1
 _____
```

②
```
   53 164
 + 31 263
 _____
```

⑤
```
   25 674
 + 35 251
 _____
```

③
```
   28 341
 + 42 025
 _____
```

⑥
```
   19 875
 + 42 312
 _____
```

④
```
   51 963
 + 26 320
 _____
```

⑦
```
   41 759
 + 16 421
 _____
```

⑧
```
   22 221
   17 316
 +  3 142
 _____
```

⑨
```
   31 372
   40 601
 +  5 414
 _____
```

⑩
```
   12 921
   23 192
 +  4 012
 _____
```

THINK Write an addition of two 5-digit numbers where every digit is different. What is the largest total you can make?

○
○ **I am confident with adding 5-digit numbers using**
○ **column addition.**

Perform these additions using the column method.

1   46 825
+ 19 041
———

3   38 421
+ 40 593
———

5   53 296
+ 46 345
———

2   52 319
+ 25 920
———

4   42 861
+ 38 412
———

6   26 139
+ 67 408
———

7   17 245
59 652
+   1 031
———

9   31 632
37 541
+   5 235
———

11   21 480
64 271
+ 17 155
———

8   62 418
13 646
+   4 101
———

10   48 217
12 426
+ 33 145
———

12   30 240
45 918
+ 27 514
———

THINK   Write an addition of two 5-digit numbers where every digit is different. What is the largest total you can make? What is the smallest total you can make? Can you make 22 221 if one of the two numbers has 4 digits?

I am confident with adding 5-digit numbers using column addition.

1
```
  48 607
− 23 425
```

Watch out! You will need to move a 100 into the 10s!

2
```
  68 049
− 54 317
```

5
```
  93 825
− 29 541
```

8
```
  65 411
− 55 920
```

3
```
  90 538
− 74 305
```

6
```
  77 029
− 59 115
```

9
```
  60 327
− 54 115
```

4
```
  48 563
− 33 207
```

7
```
  86 309
− 72 647
```

THINK

Choose the subtraction you found trickiest. Check the answer using addition.

○
○
○

I am confident with subtracting 5-digit numbers using column subtraction.

1 59 075
    − 36 429

4 69 540
    − 38 293

7 58 207
    − 39 115

2 82 607
    − 64 352

5 45 867
    − 30 991

8 65 237
    − 36 192

3 75 928
    − 57 664

6 50 390
    − 22 165

9 47 064
    − 25 337

Solve these word problems.

10 One video-sharing website has 65 382 hits. Another site has 48 247 hits. What is the difference between the numbers of hits on the two websites?

11 There are two stadiums in a city. The first has 52 468 seats and the second has 63 740. How many more seats does the second have?

12 The city of Lichfield has a population of 58 896. Nearby, Hereford has a population of 31 068. How many more people live in Lichfield?

 THINK Check your first three answers using written column addition.

I am confident with subtracting 5-digit numbers using column subtraction.

Adding and subtracting 5-digit numbers

Follow these instructions.

1 Write a 5-digit number where the first digit is larger than the last digit. For example, 47 831 would work because 4 is more than 1, but 17 354 would not work because 1 is less than 4.

2 Reverse the digits of the number and write this new number under the first number.

3 Subtract the second number from the first number and write the answer below it. Or, you may use Frog and write in the answer.

4 Reverse the digits of your answer. Write this number beneath.

5 Add the two numbers.

6 Repeat these steps at least 10 times with different starting numbers.

7 What do you notice about the patterns in the answers? Can you explain any of them?

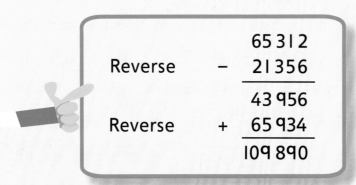

```
                        65 312
Reverse     –           21 356
                        _____
                        43 956
Reverse     +           65 934
                       _____
                       109 890
```

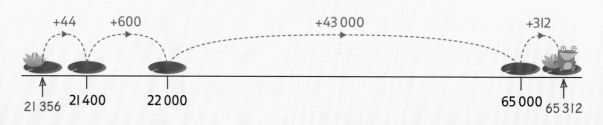

○
○ **I am confident with adding and subtracting**
○ **5-digit numbers.**

Solve these word problems.

1. Sally and Dominik were having a competition on the computer. Sally scored 82 079. Dominik scored 70 326. How much more did Sally score than Dominik?

2. The population of Hildston is 58 684. The population of Craigsville is 29 315. How many people are there in total in both towns?

3. In the latest TV talent contest, a young singer had 78 391 votes. Her rival, a gymnast, got 73 627 votes. By how many votes did the singer win?

4. A social networking site receives 65 374 hits in an hour. It is merging with another site, which gets 38 256 hits an hour. How many hits per hour can they expect to get when the sites have merged?

5. A bird called an Arctic Tern was satellite-tagged and found to fly 71 452 km in one year. The distance all the way around the world is 40 075 km. How much further than this did the bird fly in that year?

6. A Boeing 737 aeroplane weighs 70 535 kg when empty. If the mass of passengers, staff and other equipment it can carry is 19 688 kg, how much will the plane weigh when it is full?

I am confident with solving problems involving adding and subtracting 5-digit numbers.

Solve these subtractions.

Can you remember when Frog can help?

① 60 000 − 39 899 = ☐

② 70 009 − 50 945 = ☐

③ 20 300 − 9872 = ☐

④ 41 000 − 35 295 = ☐

⑤ 80 002 − 45 326 = ☐

⑥ 32 500 − 8925 = ☐

⑦ 20 006 − 12 526 = ☐

⑧ 10 010 − 2645 = ☐

⑨ 60 007 − 44 982 = ☐

⑩ 35 002 − 29 798 = ☐

⑪ 50 020 − 3775 = ☐

⑫ 42 000 − 5894 = ☐

THINK Write a 5-digit subtract 5-digit calculation where Frog needs to do only two jumps.

I am confident with subtracting from 5-digit numbers.

Choose to solve these subtractions using Frog or the column method.

Remember, if the number you are subtracting from has lots of zeros, it is better to use Frog.

1
```
  56 000
- 24 392
```

5
```
  84 372
- 68 151
```

2
```
  85 645
- 71 923
```

6
```
  90 040
- 75 319
```

3
```
  20 700
- 15 526
```

7
```
  41 000
- 39 271
```

4
```
  19 506
- 12 325
```

8
```
  27 308
- 15 026
```

Solve these word problems.

9 Mia and TJ win £24 000. They decide to buy a campervan for £16 983 to travel around the world. How much money do they have left?

10 Truro has a population of 19 382 and Wells has a population of 10 491. How many more people live in Truro?

11 A jet can fly 17 500 km without refuelling. It flies from London to Cape Town, which is 9634 km. How much further could it fly?

 **THINK** Write a word problem for your partner to solve. Choose numbers which make it obvious that they should use Frog.

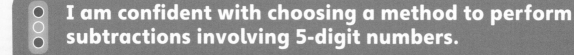
I am confident with choosing a method to perform subtractions involving 5-digit numbers.

Perform these subtractions and additions.

1
```
   26 582
 + 56 917
 _____
```

2
```
   59 672
 + 31 326
 _____
```

3
```
   75 324
 - 13 926
 _____
```

4
```
   18 940
 -  6 355
 _____
```

5
```
   48 312
 - 35 821
 _____
```

6
```
   80 320
 - 47 623
 _____
```

7
```
   44 206
   27 948
 +  1 202
 _____
```

8
```
   28 706
 - 14 921
 _____
```

 Check one of the additions using subtraction.
Check one of the subtractions using addition.

○
○ **I am confident with adding and subtracting**
○ **5-digit numbers.**

Finding factors

Copy and complete these factor trees. Then write the list of prime factors for each number.

1

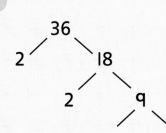

3

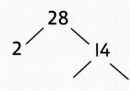

5

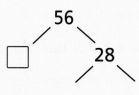

2

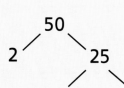

4

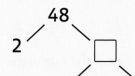

6

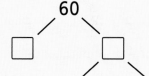

Find the prime factors of:

7 38

8 18

9 51

10 54

11 57

12 42

13 104

14 70

15 144

16 120

17 108

18 250

THINK All the numbers in questions 1–6 have 2 as a prime factor. Can you write some numbers that do not? Write a list of those that have only 2 as a prime factor, for example, 8.

○ **I am confident with working out prime factors.**

Comparing fractions

Look at the related fractions in this fraction wall.

1 whole									
$\frac{1}{2}$					$\frac{1}{2}$				
$\frac{1}{3}$			$\frac{1}{3}$			$\frac{1}{3}$			
$\frac{1}{4}$		$\frac{1}{4}$		$\frac{1}{4}$			$\frac{1}{4}$		
$\frac{1}{6}$	$\frac{1}{6}$		$\frac{1}{6}$		$\frac{1}{6}$		$\frac{1}{6}$		$\frac{1}{6}$
$\frac{1}{8}$	$\frac{1}{8}$	$\frac{1}{8}$	$\frac{1}{8}$	$\frac{1}{8}$	$\frac{1}{8}$		$\frac{1}{8}$		$\frac{1}{8}$
$\frac{1}{9}$	$\frac{1}{9}$	$\frac{1}{9}$	$\frac{1}{9}$	$\frac{1}{9}$	$\frac{1}{9}$	$\frac{1}{9}$		$\frac{1}{9}$	$\frac{1}{9}$
$\frac{1}{10}$	$\frac{1}{10}$	$\frac{1}{10}$	$\frac{1}{10}$	$\frac{1}{10}$	$\frac{1}{10}$	$\frac{1}{10}$	$\frac{1}{10}$	$\frac{1}{10}$	$\frac{1}{10}$

 **THINK** Write as many fractions as you can that are less than $\frac{1}{2}$. Each fraction must have a different denominator. Use the fraction wall to help you.

Write < or > between each pair of fractions. Write them as fractions with the same denominator first.

Use the fraction wall to help you!

1. $\frac{2}{3}$ $\frac{2}{6}$

2. $\frac{1}{3}$ $\frac{4}{9}$

3. $\frac{1}{2}$ $\frac{5}{8}$

4. $\frac{1}{4}$ $\frac{3}{8}$

5. $\frac{4}{5}$ $\frac{7}{10}$

6. $\frac{3}{4}$ $\frac{7}{8}$

○ **I am confident with comparing related fractions.**
○
○

Write each pair of fractions with the same denominator. Write < or > between each pair.

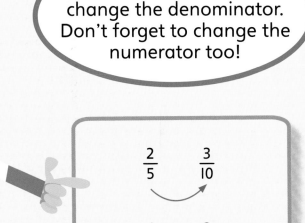

5 fits into 10 so we can change the denominator. Don't forget to change the numerator too!

$$\frac{2}{5} \qquad \frac{3}{10}$$

$$\frac{4}{10} > \frac{3}{10}$$

1. $\frac{2}{3}$ $\frac{4}{9}$

2. $\frac{4}{5}$ $\frac{3}{10}$

3. $\frac{5}{6}$ $\frac{2}{3}$

4. $\frac{3}{8}$ $\frac{1}{2}$

5. $\frac{3}{4}$ $\frac{5}{8}$

6. $\frac{1}{3}$ $\frac{2}{9}$

7. $\frac{7}{8}$ $\frac{3}{4}$

8. $\frac{7}{12}$ $\frac{3}{4}$

9. $\frac{5}{6}$ $\frac{11}{12}$

10. $\frac{2}{3}$ $\frac{7}{12}$

THINK Write three fractions where the first is half of the second and the second is half of the third. Work with a partner to write three sets of fractions like this.

I am confident with comparing related fractions.

49

Adding and subtracting fractions

Complete these additions. If the answer is more than 1, write it as a mixed number, for example, $1\frac{3}{4}$.

1 $\frac{3}{8} + \frac{5}{8} = \square$

4 $\frac{7}{8} + \frac{5}{8} = \square$

2 $\frac{3}{7} + \frac{2}{7} = \square$

5 $\frac{4}{5} + \frac{3}{5} = \square$

3 $\frac{3}{4} + \frac{3}{4} = \square$

6 $\frac{2}{3} + \frac{2}{3} = \square$

Complete these additions.
Write both fractions as eighths first.

7 $\frac{1}{4} + \frac{1}{8} = \square$

9 $\frac{5}{8} + \frac{1}{4} = \square$

8 $\frac{3}{4} + \frac{1}{8} = \square$

10 $\frac{7}{8} + \frac{2}{4} = \square$

Complete these additions.
Write both fractions as sixths first.

11 $\frac{1}{3} + \frac{1}{6} = \square$

13 $\frac{5}{6} + \frac{1}{3} = \square$

12 $\frac{2}{3} + \frac{1}{6} = \square$

14 $\frac{4}{6} + \frac{2}{3} = \square$

THINK Write two fractions with different denominators where one is double the other.

○ **I am confident with adding fractions and**
○ **mixed numbers.**
○

Complete these additions.

> If you can change the denominator it is a lot easier!

1 $\frac{2}{3} + \frac{1}{6} = \square$

2 $\frac{3}{4} + \frac{1}{8} = \square$ **4** $\frac{1}{2} + \frac{3}{8} = \square$ **6** $\frac{7}{10} + \frac{1}{5} = \square$

3 $\frac{2}{5} + \frac{3}{10} = \square$ **5** $\frac{1}{3} + \frac{1}{9} = \square$ **7** $\frac{1}{9} + \frac{2}{3} = \square$

Complete these additions. Write the answers as mixed numbers, for example, $1\frac{3}{4}$.

8 $\frac{2}{3} + \frac{5}{6} = \square$ **11** $\frac{3}{4} + \frac{5}{12} = \square$

9 $\frac{5}{8} + \frac{3}{4} = \square$ **12** $\frac{2}{3} + \frac{4}{9} = \square$

10 $\frac{1}{3} + \frac{7}{9} = \square$ **13** $\frac{7}{12} + \frac{2}{3} = \square$

THINK   Write an addition of two fractions, each with a different denominator, where the answer is exactly 1. Write two more pairs.

I am confident with adding fractions and mixed numbers

Choose pairs of fractions to add.

$$\frac{2}{5} \qquad \frac{3}{4}$$

$$\frac{1}{3} \qquad \frac{1}{4} \qquad \frac{3}{8}$$

$$\frac{2}{9} \qquad \frac{2}{3} \qquad \frac{5}{6}$$

$$\frac{7}{10} \qquad \frac{3}{5} \qquad \frac{3}{10}$$

Find three pairs of fractions with a total of more than 1. Then find three pairs with a total of less than 1.

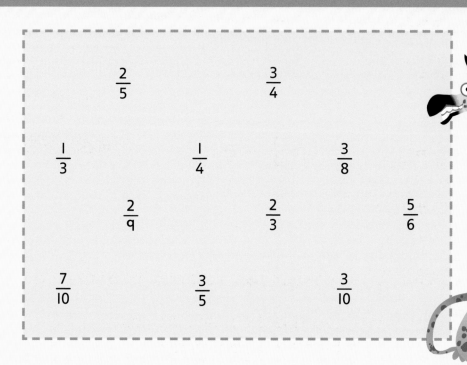

$$\frac{2}{5} \qquad \frac{3}{4}$$

$$\frac{1}{3} \qquad \frac{1}{4} \qquad \frac{3}{8}$$

$$\frac{2}{9} \qquad \frac{2}{3} \qquad \frac{5}{6}$$

$$\frac{7}{10} \qquad \frac{3}{5} \qquad \frac{3}{10}$$

I am confident with adding fractions and mixed numbers.

Subtract these groups of fractions with related denominators.

① $\dfrac{5}{6} - \dfrac{2}{3} = \square$ ③ $\dfrac{1}{3} - \dfrac{1}{6} = \square$

② $\dfrac{2}{3} - \dfrac{1}{6} = \square$

Write the fractions so that the denominators match.

④ $\dfrac{7}{8} - \dfrac{3}{4} = \square$ ⑥ $\dfrac{7}{8} - \dfrac{1}{4} = \square$

⑤ $\dfrac{5}{8} - \dfrac{1}{4} = \square$

⑦ $\dfrac{9}{10} - \dfrac{1}{5} = \square$ ⑨ $\dfrac{4}{5} - \dfrac{3}{10} = \square$

⑧ $\dfrac{7}{10} - \dfrac{2}{5} = \square$

⑩ $\dfrac{2}{3} - \dfrac{1}{9} = \square$ ⑫ $\dfrac{7}{9} - \dfrac{1}{3} = \square$

⑪ $\dfrac{8}{9} - \dfrac{2}{3} = \square$

⑬ $\dfrac{1}{2} - \dfrac{1}{8} = \square$ ⑮ $\dfrac{1}{2} - \dfrac{3}{8} = \square$

⑭ $\dfrac{1}{2} - \dfrac{1}{6} = \square$

 **THINK**   Write three of your own subtractions of the form $\dfrac{1}{2} - \dfrac{\square}{\square}$.

What sorts of fractions are easy to subtract from one-half?

I am confident with subtracting fractions with related denominators.

Subtract these fractions with related denominators.

1 $\dfrac{1}{2} - \dfrac{1}{8} = \square$

4 $\dfrac{7}{8} - \dfrac{1}{2} = \square$

2 $\dfrac{1}{2} - \dfrac{1}{6} = \square$

5 $\dfrac{7}{8} - \dfrac{1}{4} = \square$

3 $\dfrac{1}{2} - \dfrac{1}{12} = \square$

6 $\dfrac{7}{8} - \dfrac{3}{4} = \square$

Subtract these fractions.

7 $\dfrac{5}{6} - \dfrac{2}{3} = \square$

10 $\dfrac{9}{12} - \dfrac{1}{2} = \square$

13 $\dfrac{3}{4} - \dfrac{5}{12} = \square$

8 $\dfrac{5}{8} - \dfrac{1}{4} = \square$

11 $\dfrac{5}{12} - \dfrac{1}{3} = \square$

14 $\dfrac{11}{12} - \dfrac{2}{3} = \square$

9 $\dfrac{2}{3} - \dfrac{1}{9} = \square$

12 $\dfrac{7}{9} - \dfrac{1}{3} = \square$

15 $\dfrac{9}{10} - \dfrac{1}{5} = \square$

Describe how you could work out $\dfrac{2}{3} - \dfrac{1}{2}$.

Repeat this for $\dfrac{2}{3} - \dfrac{1}{4}$.

I am confident with subtracting fractions with related denominators.

54

Short division

Solve these divisions.
Write any remainder as a fraction.

1 4⟌542

2 4⟌732

3 4⟌239

4 4⟌341

Solve these questions.
Write any remainder as a fraction.

5 6⟌721

6 6⟌863

7 6⟌521

8 6⟌444

9 7⟌928

10 7⟌750

11 7⟌583

12 7⟌472

13 8⟌924

14 8⟌565

15 8⟌441

16 8⟌607

Solve these word problems.

17 The school canteen needs to make enough cottage pie to feed 244 children. A tray of cottage pie feeds 8 children. How many trays do they need to make?

18 The school canteen needs to make enough milkshake for the 197 children. One jug holds enough milkshake for 5 children. How many jugs do they need to make?

 **THINK** Complete the division 28 ☐ ÷ 6 so that the answer will be a mixed number that includes the fraction $\frac{1}{3}$.

○
○ **I am confident with using short division and writing**
○ **remainders as fractions.**

Solve these divisions. Write the remainders as fractions.

1 $3\overline{)437}$ **4** $5\overline{)652}$ **7** $7\overline{)916}$

2 $4\overline{)914}$ **5** $6\overline{)743}$ **8** $3\overline{)838}$

3 $2\overline{)739}$ **6** $4\overline{)861}$ **9** $4\overline{)1058}$

Find divisions of 3-digit numbers by 1-digit numbers that will give these answers.

10 $47\frac{3}{4}$ **12** $56\frac{4}{5}$ **14** $148\frac{1}{3}$

11 $38\frac{2}{3}$ **13** $117\frac{5}{6}$ **15** $157\frac{1}{4}$

 **THINK** Check if 256 gives a remainder of 1 when divided by 3. Investigate how many numbers between 200 and 300 also give a remainder of 1 when divided by 3. How many give a remainder of 2? Investigate how many give different remainders when divided by 4 or 5.

● ● ● **I am confident with using short division and writing remainders as fractions.**

Work out these divisions. Give any remainders as whole numbers.

1. 6 ⟌ 7484

4. 7 ⟌ 9285

7. 8 ⟌ 9204

2. 4 ⟌ 5863

5. 3 ⟌ 4750

8. 7 ⟌ 5765

3. 9 ⟌ 5863

6. 6 ⟌ 7071

9. 8 ⟌ 2863

Solve these word problems.

10. How many packs of 4 buns can be made from these numbers of buns? How many buns would be left over?

    a) 4562 buns   b) 7287 buns   c) 6541 buns

11. How many packs of 6 buns can be made from these numbers of buns? How many buns would be left over?

    a) 9857 buns   b) 7107 buns   c) 8602 buns

12. How many packs of 8 buns can be made from these numbers of buns? How many buns would be left over?

    a) 9326 buns   b) 9115 buns   c) 8916 buns

THINK Choose three divisions from this page. Check your answers using multiplication.

I am confident with dividing 4-digit numbers, leaving remainders.

Solve these word problems. Say how many cards would be left over in each case.

1 How many packs of 3 trading cards can be made from these numbers of cards?

    a) 5263 cards   b) 1345 cards   c) 4220 cards

2 How many packs of 4 trading cards can be made from these numbers of cards?

    a) 6253 cards   b) 3734 cards   c) 4185 cards

3 How many packs of 6 trading cards can be made from these numbers of cards?

    a) 8362 cards   b) 5363 cards   c) 6619 cards

4 How many packs of 8 trading cards can be made from these numbers of cards?

    a) 9369 cards   b) 6234 cards   c) 5644 cards

5 How many packs of 7 trading cards can be made from these numbers of cards?

    a) 8352 cards   b) 5239 cards   c) 7468 cards

 **THINK** Write a division ☐☐☐☐ ÷ ☐ with a remainder of 7.

I am confident with dividing 4-digit numbers, with remainders.

Multiplying 3- and 4-digit numbers

Look at this table. It shows how many of each item was sold during a three-day rock festival. Then answer the questions below.

	Day 1	Day 2	Day 3
T-shirts (£17)	364	441	578
Hats (£12)	462	556	715
Souvenir CD (£18)	128	379	608

1 Work out how much money the T-shirt stall made on each day.

Day 1: 364 × 17 = ☐

×	300	60	4
10	3000	600	40
7	2100	420	28

3640
+ 2548 = ☐

2 Work out how much money the hat stall made on each day.

3 Work out how much money the CD stall made on each day.

THINK Which of these do you think will have the bigger answer? Why?

443 × 13   318 × 19

Work them out and see if you were right.

○
○ **I am confident with multiplying 3-digit numbers**
○ **using the grid method.**

This table shows how many of each item was sold during a three-day rock festival. Answer the questions below the table. Estimate your answers first, then work them out.

	Day 1	Day 2	Day 3
Fold-up chairs (£16)	322	467	1246
Giant umbrellas (£13)	563	879	2182
Solar-powered phone chargers (£12)	835	1257	3683

1 Work out how much money the fold-up chair stall made on each day.

Day 1: 322 × 16 = ☐

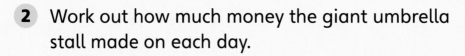

```
      3  2  2
   ×     1  6
   3  2  2  0
 + ☐  ☐  ☐  ☐
   ☐  ☐  ☐  ☐
```

2 Work out how much money the giant umbrella stall made on each day.

3 Work out how much money the solar-powered phone charger stall made on each day.

THINK What is the missing digit in this multiplication?

412 ☐ × 14 = 57 736

○
○ I am confident with multiplying 3-digit and 4-digit
○ numbers using long multiplication.

People at a rock festival were given three booklets of vouchers when they entered. Work out how many vouchers were given out per hour.

Booklet of 12
ice-cream vouchers

Booklet of 15
water vouchers

Booklet of 16
juice vouchers

Time	Number of people
12 pm – 1 pm	4231
1 pm – 2 pm	6527
2 pm – 3 pm	2434

Ice-cream vouchers from 12 pm to 1 pm

$4231 \times 12 = \square$

```
        4  2  3  1
   ×          1  2
   ─────────────────
     4  2  3  1  0
   + □  □  □  □  □
   ─────────────────
     □  □  □  □  □
```

THINK

Use the digits 2, 3, 4, 5 and 6 to make a multiplication $\square\square\square\square \times 1\square$. Try to make the biggest possible answer and the smallest possible answer.

I am confident with multiplying 4-digit numbers using long multiplication.

This table shows the monthly mileage driven by a range of bus drivers.

Driver	Monthly mileage
Alf	4983
Lucy	2648
Suzie	7553
Sandeep	3759
Raymond	8136
Isaiah	9254
Andrew	6613
Mia	8496

Estimate the mileage for each bus driver over 18 months and then work out the answer.

 THINK

Find the missing digit.

42 ☐ 6 × 18 = 76 248

○
○ **I am confident with multiplying 4-digit numbers using**
○ **long multiplication.**

Multiplication and division

Solve these divisions.

1 3)472

4 5)6257

2 4)158

5 6)8238

3 6)729

6 4)3279

Perform these multiplications.

7
```
    327
×    16
_____
```

10
```
   2341
×    12
_____
```

8
```
    472
×    12
_____
```

11
```
   4279
×    14
_____
```

9
```
    635
×    13
_____
```

12
```
   3524
×    16
_____
```

 **THINK**   Write a division with an answer of 146 r 2.

○
○   **I am confident with dividing and multiplying 3-digit**
○   **and 4-digit numbers.**

Area and perimeter

Calculate the area and perimeter of these rectangles.

> Remember that area is measured in square centimetres (cm²) and perimeter is measured in centimetres (cm).

1

3 cm

5 cm

4

8 cm

3 cm

2

6 cm

4 cm

5

12 cm

2 cm

3

7 cm

5 cm

6

6 cm

6 cm

THINK Write the perimeter of: a rectangle measuring 7 cm by 6 cm, a square with a side of 8 cm, and a square with an area of 25 cm².

I am confident with finding the area and perimeter of squares and rectangles.

Calculate the area and perimeter of these gardens.

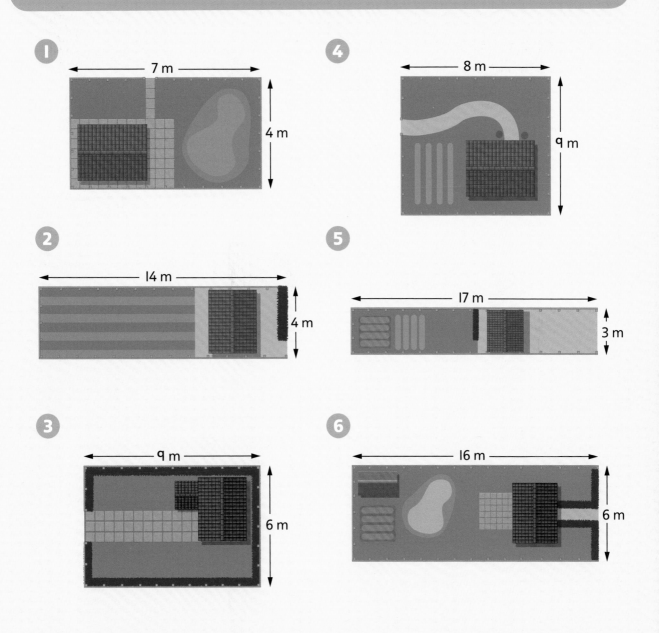

1. 7 m, 4 m

2. 14 m, 4 m

3. 9 m, 6 m

4. 8 m, 9 m

5. 17 m, 3 m

6. 16 m, 6 m

7. Each garden has a fence around its perimeter. Which garden has a fence that is twice the length of one of the other fences?

THINK Draw three rectangles with a perimeter of 12 units. Do they all have the same area?

I am confident with finding the area and perimeter of different kinds of rectangles.

65

Calculate the area of these leaves.

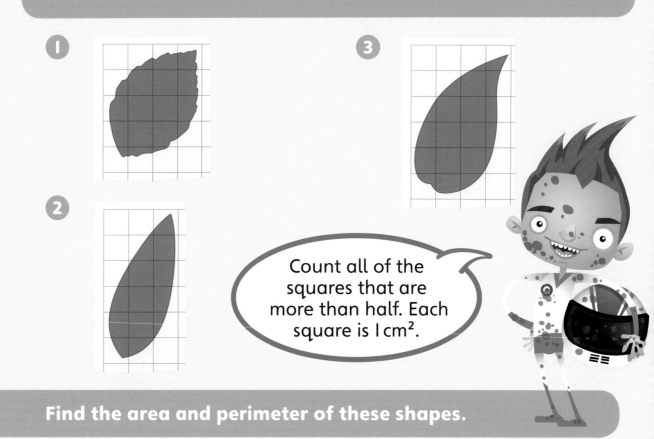

1

2

3

Count all of the squares that are more than half. Each square is 1 cm².

Find the area and perimeter of these shapes.

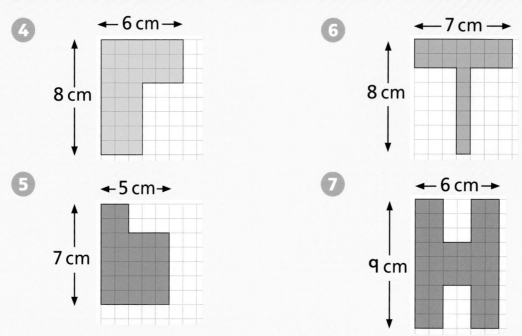

4
← 6 cm →
8 cm

5
← 5 cm →
7 cm

6
← 7 cm →
8 cm

7
← 6 cm →
9 cm

THINK Draw round your hand on squared paper, keeping your fingers together. Estimate, then find the area of your hand.

I am confident with finding the area and perimeter of irregular shapes.

Calculate the area and perimeter of these shapes.

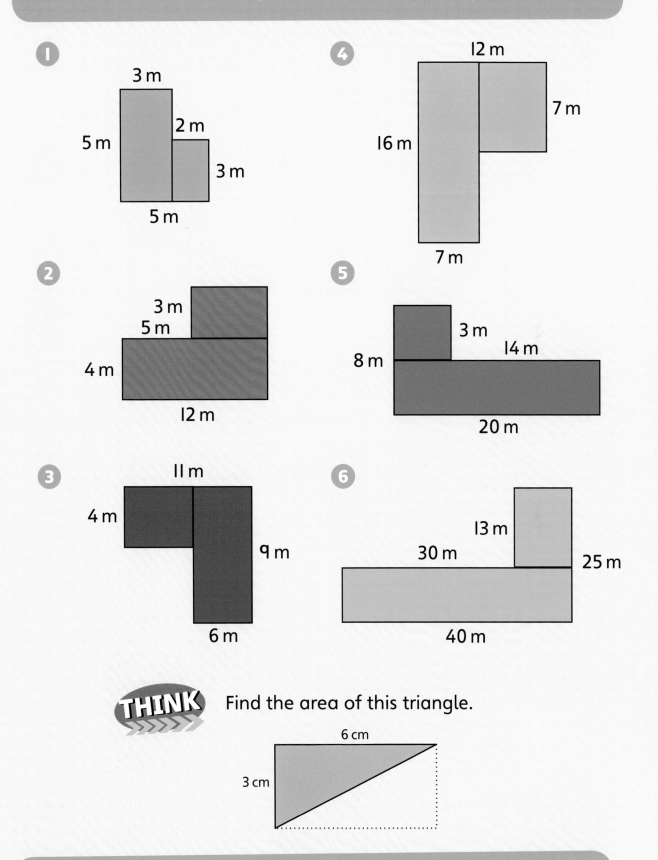

1

3 m

2 m

5 m

3 m

5 m

2

3 m

5 m

4 m

12 m

3

11 m

4 m

9 m

6 m

4

12 m

7 m

16 m

7 m

5

3 m

14 m

8 m

20 m

6

13 m

30 m

25 m

40 m

THINK   Find the area of this triangle.

6 cm

3 cm

Work out the missing lengths for each of these shapes.

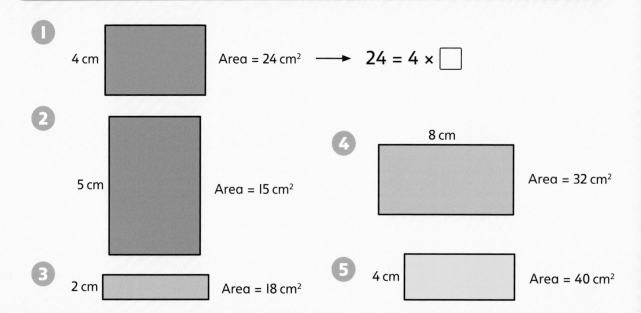

1   4 cm   Area = 24 cm² ⟶ $24 = 4 \times \square$

2   5 cm   Area = 15 cm²

4   8 cm   Area = 32 cm²

3   2 cm   Area = 18 cm²

5   4 cm   Area = 40 cm²

Work out the missing lengths for each of these shapes.

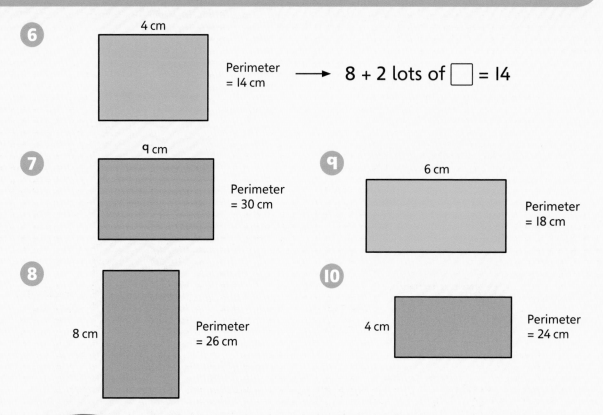

6   4 cm   Perimeter = 14 cm ⟶ $8 + 2 \text{ lots of } \square = 14$

7   9 cm   Perimeter = 30 cm

9   6 cm   Perimeter = 18 cm

8   8 cm   Perimeter = 26 cm

10   4 cm   Perimeter = 24 cm

 THINK   A rectangle has a perimeter of 14 cm and an area of 10 cm². What could its length and width be?

Work out the missing lengths and the perimeters of these shapes.

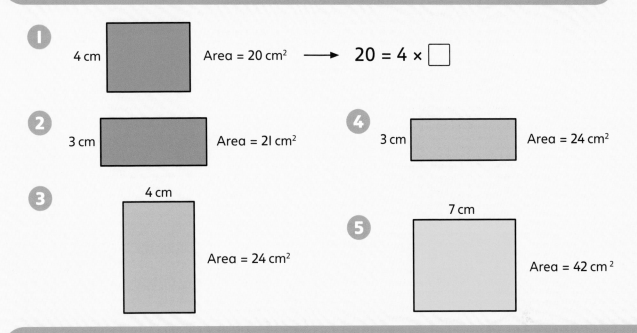

1 4 cm, Area = 20 cm² ⟶ $20 = 4 \times \square$

2 3 cm, Area = 21 cm²

4 3 cm, Area = 24 cm²

3 4 cm, Area = 24 cm²

5 7 cm, Area = 42 cm²

Work out the missing lengths and the areas of these shapes.

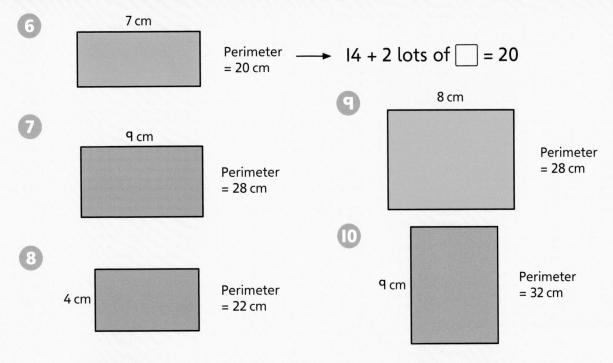

6 7 cm, Perimeter = 20 cm ⟶ $14 + 2 \text{ lots of } \square = 20$

7 9 cm, Perimeter = 28 cm

9 8 cm, Perimeter = 28 cm

8 4 cm, Perimeter = 22 cm

10 9 cm, Perimeter = 32 cm

THINK A shape has a perimeter of 20 cm and an area of 21 cm². What shape could it be? What would the lengths of the sides be?

○
○ I am confident with finding the area and perimeter
○ of shapes, and calculating missing lengths.

Volume and capacity

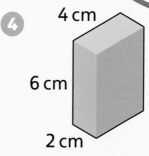

Work out the area of the base then multiply it by the height.

Calculate the volume of each cuboid.

1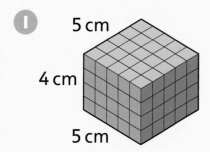
5 cm
4 cm
5 cm

4
4 cm
6 cm
2 cm

2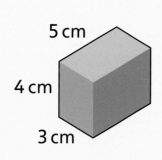
5 cm
4 cm
3 cm

5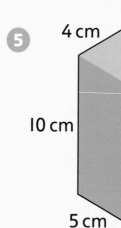
4 cm
10 cm
5 cm

3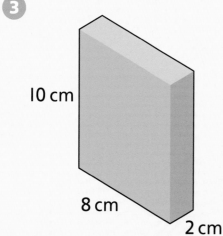
10 cm
8 cm
2 cm

6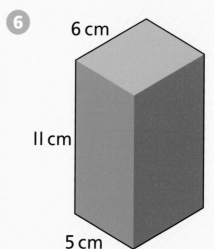
6 cm
11 cm
5 cm

THINK What length are the sides of a cube with a volume of 125 cm³?

○○○ **I am confident with calculating the volume of a cuboid.**

Work out the capacity of these containers. Give your answers in millilitres.

1 8 cm · 9 cm · 4 cm

4 12 cm · 4 cm · 2 cm

Remember that 1 cm³ = 1 ml.

2 10 cm · 6 cm · 5 cm

5 8 cm · 5 cm · 10 cm

3 3 cm · 4 cm · 11 cm

6 7 cm · 7 cm · 7 cm

 **THINK**   What could the dimensions be of a container that can hold 1 litre?

○
○ **I am confident with calculating volume and**
○ **capacity.**

Work out the area and perimeter of these shapes.

①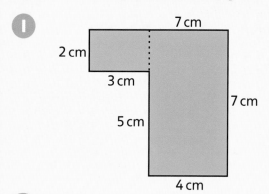
2 cm
7 cm
3 cm
5 cm
7 cm
4 cm

③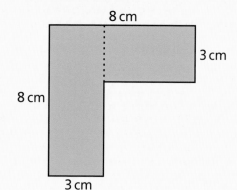
8 cm
3 cm
8 cm
3 cm

②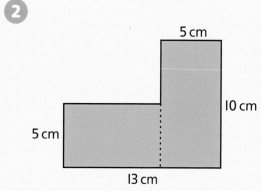
5 cm
10 cm
5 cm
13 cm

Work out the volume (cm³) and the capacity (ml) of these containers.

④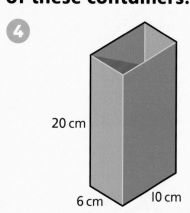
20 cm
6 cm
10 cm

⑤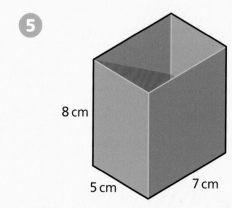
8 cm
5 cm
7 cm

 **THINK** The capacity of a cuboid is 480 ml and the area of the base is 60 cm². What is the height of the cuboid? Draw another container that would have the same capacity.

○ **I am confident with working out area, perimeter,**
○
○ **volume and capacity.**

Fractions, decimals and percentages

Write the coloured percentage of each 10 × 10 square.
Then write each percentage as a fraction.
Simplify each fraction where you can.

1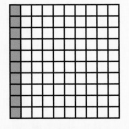

4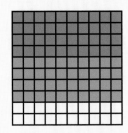

7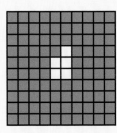

2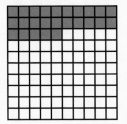

5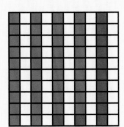

8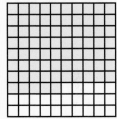

3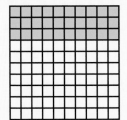

6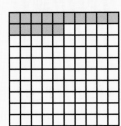

Write these fractions as percentages.

9 $\dfrac{1}{10}$

11 $\dfrac{35}{100}$

13 $\dfrac{1}{2}$

15 $\dfrac{3}{4}$

10 $\dfrac{7}{10}$

12 $\dfrac{1}{4}$

14 $\dfrac{7}{10}$

16 $\dfrac{1}{5}$

THINK Draw a 10 × 10 square. Using whole squares, colour squares to make the initial of your first name. You must colour at least 20% of the grid. Write what percentage you have coloured.

○
○ **I am confident with converting percentages**
○ **and fractions.**

Write the coloured percentage of each 10 × 10 square. Write the percentage of each square that is not coloured.

① 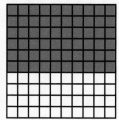   ③ 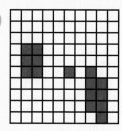   ⑤ 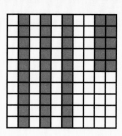   ⑦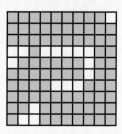

② 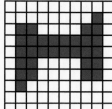   ④ 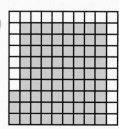   ⑥ 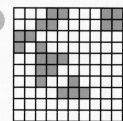   ⑧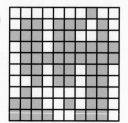

Write these fractions as percentages.

⑨ $\dfrac{80}{100}$ ⑪ $\dfrac{45}{100}$ ⑬ $\dfrac{1}{100}$ ⑮ $\dfrac{1}{4}$ ⑰ $\dfrac{1}{5}$

⑩ $\dfrac{10}{100}$ ⑫ $\dfrac{95}{100}$ ⑭ $\dfrac{1}{2}$ ⑯ $\dfrac{3}{4}$ ⑱ $\dfrac{7}{10}$

Write these percentages as two different fractions.

⑲ 30%   ㉑ 90%   ㉓ 10%   ㉕ 70%

⑳ 25%   ㉒ 20%   ㉔ 75%   ㉖ 110%

 Find a way to colour 20% of a 10 × 10 square so that there are no more than two squares coloured in each row or column.

I am confident with reading and converting percentages and fractions.

Write the coloured area as a fraction and as a percentage.

 1 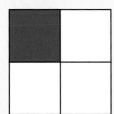 3 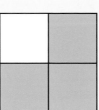 5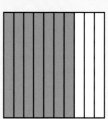

2  4  6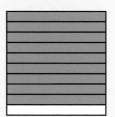

Find 50% of these amounts.
Then find 25% of these amounts.

> Remember that 50% is the same as $\frac{1}{2}$, and 25% is the same as $\frac{1}{4}$!

7 £40   9 £20   11 £24

8 £60   10 £80   12 £36

Find 10%, then 20% and then 30% of these amounts.

13 £30   14 £50   15 £25

> Remember that $\frac{1}{10}$ is the same as 10%!

 **THINK**   Which is more:
10% of £80 or 25% of £40?

Find 10% of each amount in this table. Then use these numbers to help you find the other percentages for each amount.

1.

Amount	10%	20%	30%	40%	50%	60%	70%	80%	90%	15%
£50										
£120										
£70										
£25										

Find 50% of these amounts. Then use your answers to help you find 75% of each amount.

Remember that 50% is the same as $\frac{1}{2}$, and 75% is the same as $\frac{3}{4}$!

2. £60

4. £72

3. £48

5. £30

Solve this word problem.

6. James won £800. He chose to give 50% of the amount to charity and one-quarter of the amount to his son. How much was he left with and what percentage of the original amount was this?

THINK Tom says that his survey of cats shows that 4 out of 5 prefer fish to meat and the rest prefer meat to fish. Rosie says that this means that 40% prefer meat. Is she correct?

I am confident with calculating percentages that are multiples of 10.

Complete the table and use it to help you answer the questions below.

1

Amount	50%	25%	75%	10%	5%	1%
£80						
£120						
£60						

2 52% of £80

3 90% of £80

4 85% of £80

5 23% of £120

6 60% of £120

7 74% of £120

8 49% of £60

9 65% of £60

10 19% of £60

Write the new prices in the sale.

11
Was £40
50% off

13
Was £60
10% off

15
Was £100
5% off

17
Was £50
60% off

12
Was £50
20% off

14
Was £80
25% off

16
Was £20
40% off

18
Was £40
15% off

Solve these word problems.

19 Rama spends 30% of his day sleeping, 25% at school, 10% watching television and 10% eating. How many hours does he have left for other activities?

20 In a book sale, all books have 50% off. Natalie buys four books with original prices of £4·50, £1·60, £12·80 and £3·40. How much does she save?

I am confident with calculating percentages.

Write each coloured part as a fraction, a percentage and a decimal.

> Write each fraction as hundredths before writing the decimal and percentage.

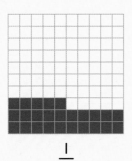

① $\frac{1}{4}$

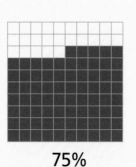

③ 75%

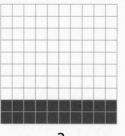

⑤ $\frac{2}{10}$

② $\frac{1}{10}$

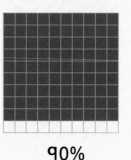

④ 90%

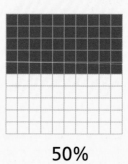

⑥ 50%

Write these as decimals.

⑦ $\frac{8}{10}$ **⑨** $\frac{21}{100}$ **⑪** $\frac{86}{100}$ **⑬** $\frac{7}{100}$

⑧ $\frac{9}{10}$ **⑩** $\frac{37}{100}$ **⑫** $\frac{1}{100}$ **⑭** $\frac{121}{100}$

Write these as hundredths.

⑮ 0.9   **⑰** 0.35   **⑲** 0.60   **㉑** 0.23

⑯ 0.2   **⑱** 0.89   **⑳** 0.11   **㉒** 0.56

THINK If seven in every ten teenagers have a mobile phone, is it true that 40% do not?

○
○ **I am confident with calculating and comparing**
○ **fractions, decimals and percentages.**

1.

Fraction	$\frac{1}{2}$		$\frac{1}{10}$		$\frac{1}{5}$	$\frac{2}{5}$		$\frac{1}{50}$
Percentage		25%			20%		1%	2%
Decimal	0·5			0·75		0·4		

I am a number. What am I?

2. I am 50% of a quarter of 32.

3. I am two-thirds of 60% of £50.

4. I am exactly half-way between 25% of 80 cm and 40% of 120 cm.

5. I am one-quarter of 50% of 88 kg.

6. I am 3% of half of £600.

7. I am exactly half-way between one-fifth of 25 cm and 2% of 300 cm.

8. I am greater than 0·6 kg, less than one-third of 6 kg, and equal to four times 10% of 3 kg.

 You pay £20 for a hoody in a sale. It had been reduced by 50%. What was the original price? What would the original price be if it had been reduced by 75%?

I am confident with calculating and comparing fractions, decimals and percentages.

Equivalent fractions and percentages

Look at the coloured grid.

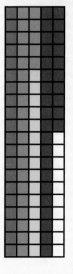

1. What fraction of the grid is red?

2. What percentage of the grid is yellow?

3. Is the purple area of the grid greater or less than 40%?

4. Which colour is 20% of the grid?

5. What colour is exactly $\frac{1}{4}$ of the grid?

6. Write the non-coloured part of the grid as a decimal.

Look at the cats and answer the questions.

What fraction of the cats:

7. are ginger?

8. have collars?

9. have a bell?

10. are not black?

11. Write each fraction as a percentage and as a decimal.

 **THINK** Write three percentages that represent an amount between $\frac{1}{4}$ and 0·4.

○
○ **I am confident with equivalent fractions and**
○ **percentages.**

1. There are 60 cats. One-quarter prefer chicken cat food, the rest prefer fish. What percentage prefer fish?

2. In a class of 30 children, 40% have packed lunches and the rest have school dinners. What fraction has school dinners?

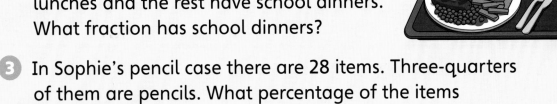

3. In Sophie's pencil case there are 28 items. Three-quarters of them are pencils. What percentage of the items are not pencils?

4. Of 40 football players at a club, seven-tenths were born in the UK. What percentage of the players were not born in the UK?

5. A fish tank contains 80 fish. 60% of the fish are angelfish. What fraction are not angelfish?

6. There are 120 photos in an album. One-quarter of the photos were taken before 2010. What percentage of the photos were taken in or after 2010?

7. In a street of 120 houses, 95% have satellite dishes. What fraction of the houses do not have satellite dishes? How many houses is this?

8. At a florist's shop, 55% of the people who buy flowers are female and the rest are male. What fraction of the buyers are male?

THINK There are 200 children in School A. 75% have school dinners. There are 300 children in School B. 50% have school dinners. Which school has to make more dinners?

Roman numerals

Look at the timeline and write the date of each event in Roman numerals.

— 1700

1 — 1791 – Charles Babbage born

2 — 1822 – Babbage proposed the idea of a computing machine

3 — 1918 – Enigma machine invented

4 — 1936 – First programmable computer

5 — 1961 – First electronic calculator

6 — 1971 – First email sent

7 — 1981 – First laptop

8 — 1982 – Internet invented

9 — 1991 – World Wide Web used by public

10 — 1995 – First online auction site set up

11 — 1997 – BBC website launched

12 — 2007 – BBC iplayer launched

— 2010

THINK Not everyone agrees with the date of the first computer. Some people say it was invented six years later. What year would this have been? Give your answer in Roman numerals.

○
○ **I am confident with reading and writing Roman**
○ **numerals.**

Finding cube numbers

Sunil is making larger cubes out of interlocking cubes. Work out how many interlocking cubes he needs to make each model.

1 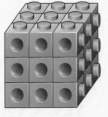 $2^3 = 2 \times 2 \times 2 = \square$

Remember, you can write 3^3 as $3 \times 3 \times 3$ and 4^3 as $4 \times 4 \times 4$.

2 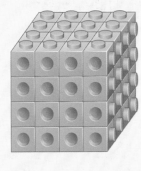 $3^3 = \square$

4 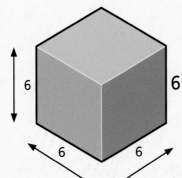 $5^3 = \square$

3 $4^3 = \square$

5 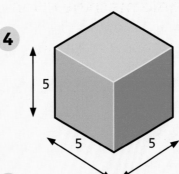 $6^3 = \square$

6 Work out how many cubes will be needed to make the next four large cubes in the pattern.

THINK Which of these cube numbers are also square numbers?

○ **I am confident with finding cube numbers.**

Drawing and reading line graphs

Copy the table and extend it up to £10. Then use this data to draw and mark a line graph marking the horizontal axis up to £10. Use the graph to convert the prices.

x-axis (£)	1	2	3	4
y-axis (rupees)	80	160	240	

1  800 R

4  480 R

7  1200 R

2 240 R

5  360 R

8  4000 R

3  440 R

6  1600 R

9  200 R

How much will you get in rupees for:

10 £3?

12 £10?

14 £40?

11 £5?

13 £15?

THINK Use your line graph to find out how many rupees you would get for £1·50, £2·50, and some other amounts between those plotted on your graph.

○
○ **I am confident with drawing and interpreting**
○ **line graphs.**

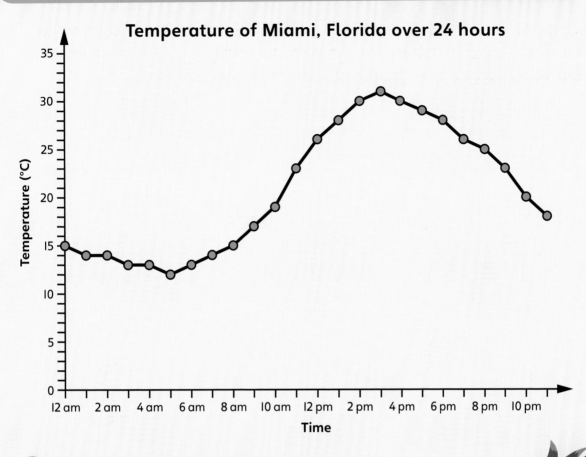

Temperature of Miami, Florida over 24 hours

1. What was the temperature at 1 am?

2. What was the temperature at 11 am?

3. What was the temperature at 2 pm?

4. What was the temperature at 9 pm?

5. How much warmer was it at 6 pm than 6 am?

6. At what time was the temperature hottest?
   At what time was it coolest?

7. What was the hottest temperature of the day?
   What was the coolest?

 How do you think a line graph might look different for a winter's day in this country?

○ **I am confident with reading line graphs.**

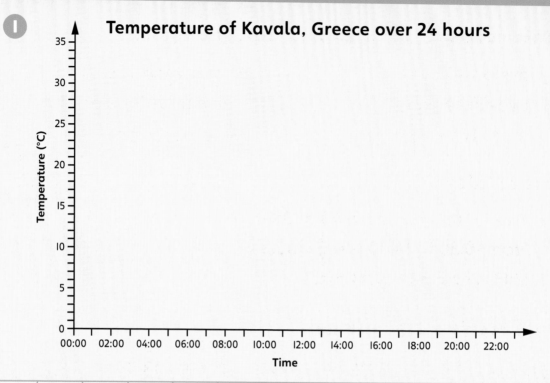

Temperature of Kavala, Greece over 24 hours

Time	00:00	02:00	04:00	06:00	08:00	10:00	12:00	14:00	16:00	18:00	20:00	22:00
Temp °C	20	19	17	17	21	23	26	32	35	33	29	25

Look at the graph and answer these questions.

2 What is the temperature at 10 am?

3 What is the difference between the temperatures at 6 am and 6 pm?

4 What is the difference between the temperatures at 7 am and 7 pm?

5 Estimate the lowest temperature and between which two times it might have occurred.

 Sketch two line graphs to show how you think the temperature might change over a day where you live, one in winter and one in summer.

I am confident with creating and reading line graphs.

Reading timetables

Write each time using 24-hour clock notation.

1. five past 7 pm
2. two-fifteen am
3. six forty-two pm
4. twenty-five past 8 pm
5. nine fifty-three am
6. half past 4 pm

True or false?

7. Twenty to 4 can be 15:40 or 3:40.
8. From 10:30 to 14:00 is $4\frac{1}{2}$ hours.
9. 13:13 is around lunchtime.

Look at this bus timetable.

Whitby	08:59	11:27	14:19	18:19
Robin-Hood's Bay	09:17	11:45	14:37	18:37
Cloughton	09:38	12:06	14:58	18:58
Scarborough	10:10	12:38	15:30	19:30

10. At what time does the bus leaving Whitby at about 9 am reach Scarborough?

11. Jo leaves Robin-Hood's Bay at quarter to midday. At what time does she reach Cloughton?

12. How long does the bus leaving Cloughton at two minutes to 7 in the evening take to reach Scarborough?

 THINK A train leaves between 10 am and 11 am. It takes 30 minutes to get to its destination. It arrives between 11:05 and 11:35. At what possible times ending in '5' or '0' could it have started?

 I am confident with using 12-hour and 24-hour clock times, and reading timetables.

Read the timetable and solve the problems. Write your answers using 24-hour clock times.

London	Ashford	Lille	Brussels
06:10	06:59	07:56	08:37
07:43	–	–	09:58
08:39	09:30	10:26	11:08
10:43	–	12:24	12:05
12:41	13:30	14:29	15:10
14:42	–	16:21	17:02
16:39	17:29	18:29	19:10
18:11	–	19:56	20:37

1 You arrive at the station in London at 07:53. How long do you have to wait for the next train?

2 You leave London on the train at 08:39. At what time do you get to Lille? How long does it take you?

3 You leave Ashford on the 09:30 train. At what time do you get to Brussels? How long does it take you?

4 If you need to be in Brussels at 12:00 which trains could you take from London?

5 What is the shortest time between trains at Lille?

6 Which of the trains takes the shortest time to travel from London to Brussels?

 **THINK** What do you notice about the times 12:51 and 15:12? Think of a similar pair of times and use Frog to find the difference between them.

○
○ **I am confident with using timetables and**
○ **24-hour clocks.**

Look at this old timetable. A new, faster aeroplane has been introduced which will reduce all these flight times by a tenth. Work out the new arrival times if flights take off at the same departure times.

Flight	From... to...	Departure time	Arrival time
BA7462	LGW to SKG	09:50	12:50
TOM2344	LHR to ATH	09:35	13:15
RA7171	STN to CDG	12:10	13:50
EJ2922	LGW to MAD	15:22	17:42
TOM6243	STN to KVA	16:55	19:05
MA4505	LGW to FRA	22:50	00:40

Jack's train journey lasts 42 minutes.
He leaves after 10 am and arrives after 11 am.
If his train leaves on a multiple of 5 minutes, what possible times could it leave and arrive?

 I am confident with using timetables and 12- and 24-hour clocks.

Scaling

A factory is making scale models of dinosaurs. Each model needs to be $\frac{1}{10}$ of the actual measurement of the dinosaur. Work out what dimensions the models need to be.

1 2.9 m, 7.9 m

2 4.3 m, 8.5 m

3 0.8 m, 1.8 m

4 7 m, 15.2 m

5 9.1 m, 27.1 m

6 15.2 m, 30.5 m

THINK The Eiffel Tower is 324 m tall. What would be a reasonable size for a scale model to be made in the classroom? What fraction of the actual height would this be?

○
○   **I am confident with using scaling to find**
○   **new dimensions.**
○

Using factors to multiply

Perform these calculations.

1. Work out 10 × 420.
   Use this to work out 5 × 420 and 20 × 420.

2. Work out 3 × 35.
   Use this to work out 6 × 35, 9 × 35 and 30 × 35.

3. Work out 100 × 28.
   Use this to work out 50 × 28 and 25 × 28.

4. Work out 2 × 47.
   Use this to work out 4 × 47 and 8 × 47.

5. Work out 4 × 31.
   Use this to work out 4 × 62, 8 × 31 and 4 × 124.

6. Work out 3 × 44.
   Use this to work out 3 × 88, 6 × 44 and 3 × 132.

7. Work out 10 × 365.
   Use this to work out 5 × 365, 20 × 365 and 25 × 365.

 **THINK** Write instructions to show someone a quick way to multiply a number by 5, then by 9 and then by 50.

○
○ **I am confident with using factors to multiply.**
○

A toy factory makes different toys at different rates. Work out how many of each toy the factory makes in an 8-hour shift. Then work out how many they would make in 24 hours.

1 Teddy bears are made at a rate of 28 an hour.

8-hour shift = ☐   24 hours = ☐

2 Robo-pets are made at a rate of 7 an hour.

8-hour shift = ☐   24 hours = ☐

3 Juggling balls are made at a rate of 46 sets an hour.

8-hour shift = ☐   24 hours = ☐

4 Toy cars are made at a rate of 18 an hour.

8-hour shift = ☐   24 hours = ☐

How many minutes does it take to fill each container?

5

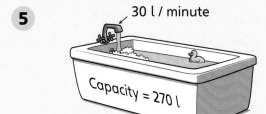

30 l / minute

Capacity = 270 l

7

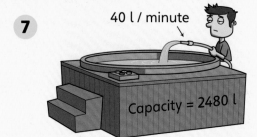

40 l / minute

Capacity = 2480 l

6

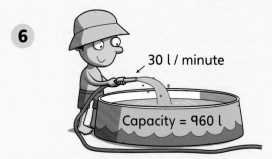

30 l / minute

Capacity = 960 l

8

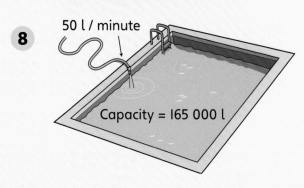

50 l / minute

Capacity = 165 000 l

THINK Write the answers to questions 7 and 8 in hours and minutes. Write the answer to question 8 in days and hours.

○ **I am confident with using factors to multiply.**

Mixed problems

Solve these word problems.

1 A toy fish tank has a height of 10 cm and a length and width of 10 cm by 8 cm. What is the area of the base? How much water does the tank hold? Remember, capacity is measured in ml, and 1 cm³ = 1 ml.

2 A train leaves Manchester at 18:25. It takes 3 hours and 15 minutes to reach its destination. At what time does it arrive?

3 A 2D shape has been drawn on a coordinate grid. The coordinates are: (2, 3), (2, 4), (5, 4), (6, 3). What sort of shape is it? Write the new coordinates of the shape when it has been reflected in the y-axis.

4 A pizza delivery outlet serves 2075 orders per week. The average price of an order is £16. How much money do they make in a week? It costs £9868 per week to run the shop and make the pizzas. How much profit do they make?

5 A pilot flies from London to Paris and back, which is a total of 437 miles. She does this journey five times. How many miles more than 2000 has she flown altogether?

6 Jameel had £43·90 in his money box but spent £29·15 of it. Katie had £54·60 in her money box but spent £39·90 of it. Who has more money after their spending? How much do they each have?

7 A coach takes 2 hours and 18 minutes to reach its destination. If it arrives at 14:14, at what time did it leave? Write your answer so that it includes the word 'midday'.

○○○ **I am confident with choosing and using a method to solve a word problem.**

Solve these calculations.

1 £2·40 + £3·99 + 50p = ☐

2 $\frac{2}{5} + \frac{3}{10} =$ ☐

3
$$\begin{array}{r} 44 \\ \times\ 13 \\ \hline \end{array}$$

4 Find 50% of £68.

5 Find 75% of £72.

6
$$\begin{array}{r} 28\,341 \\ +\ 42\,025 \\ \hline \end{array}$$

7
$$\begin{array}{r} 68\,049 \\ -\ 54\,317 \\ \hline \end{array}$$

8
$$\begin{array}{r} 168 \\ \times\ 13 \\ \hline \end{array}$$

9
$$\begin{array}{r} 20\,700 \\ -\ 15\,526 \\ \hline \end{array}$$

10 $\frac{8}{9} - \frac{2}{3} =$ ☐

11 $6\overline{)444}$

12 $9\overline{)5863}$

13 322 x 5 = ☐

14 $4 \times \frac{3}{10} =$ ☐

15
$$\begin{array}{r} 124 \\ \times\ 14 \\ \hline \end{array}$$

16 $\frac{5}{8} \times 3 =$ ☐

17 $\frac{2}{3} - \frac{1}{9} =$ ☐

18
$$\begin{array}{r} 31\,372 \\ 40\,601 \\ +\ \ 5\,414 \\ \hline \end{array}$$

19
$$\begin{array}{r} 93\,825 \\ -\ 55\,920 \\ \hline \end{array}$$

20
$$\begin{array}{r} 877 \\ \times\ 18 \\ \hline \end{array}$$

21
$$\begin{array}{r} 41\,000 \\ -\ 39\,271 \\ \hline \end{array}$$

22 2145 x 4 = ☐

23 $8\overline{)607}$

24 $6\overline{)7071}$

25 Rakesh and Jo play a computer game. Rakesh scored 82 079. Jo scored 70 745. How much more did Rakesh score than Jo?

26 At a theme park the entrance fees are £6 for a child and £11·50 for an adult. Rides cost £4 each. If a man and his 10-year-old son have £50 to spend in total, how many rides can they go on after paying the entrance fees?

cube products

Read numbers up, across, or diagonally to find 3-digit numbers on this cube. Then use a written method to multiply each number by 6, 7 or 8.

1 What is the largest product you can find?

2 What is the smallest product you can find?

Can you find multiplications with a product:

3 greater than 7000?

4 close to 5000?

5 that end in the digits 12?

6 that has three digits the same?

**Choose more 3-digit numbers from the cube.
Use a written method to multiply these by 12, 13 or 14.**

Can you find multiplications with a product:

7 between 11 000 and 12 000?

8 close to 3000?

9 that end in the digits 96?

10 that has at least one zero digit?

11 Are there two products that have a difference of 253?

Series Editor
Ruth Merttens

Author Team
Jennie Kerwin and Hilda Merttens

Published by Pearson Education Limited, Edinburgh Gate, Harlow, Essex, CM20 2JE.

www.pearsonschools.co.uk

Text © Pearson Education Limited 2014
Page design and layout by room9design
Original illustrations © Pearson Education Limited 2014
Illustrated by Marek Jagucki pp4–5, 7–10, 12–13, 18, 20–21, 27, 43, 45, 55, 57–58, 61–62, 77–78, 80–82, 84, 89–90, 92–93; Matt Buckley pp24–25, 28–37, 42, 65–66, 67–72, 83, 85–86, 95; Bill Ledger pp8
Cover design by Pearson Education Limited
Cover photo/illustration by Volker Beisler © Pearson Education Limited
Additional contributions by Hilary Koll and Steve Mills, CME Projects Ltd.

First published 2014

16
10 9 8 7 6 5 4

British Library Cataloguing in Publication Data
A catalogue record for this book is available from the British Library

ISBN 978 1 408 27855 0

Copyright notice

Printed in Slovakia by Neografia

Acknowledgements
We would like to thank the staff and pupils at North Kidlington Primary School, Haydon Wick Primary School, Swindon, St Mary's Catholic Primary School, Bodmin, St Andrew's C of E Primary & Nursery School, Sutton-in-Ashfield, Saint James' C of E Primary School, Southampton and Harborne Primary School, Birmingham, for their invaluable help in the development and trialling of this book.

Every effort has been made to contact copyright holders of material reproduced in this book. Any omissions will be rectified in subsequent printings if notice is given to the publishers.